Puss in Boots

A big, bad, ugly Ogre lives in a beautiful castle.
The castle is near Daniel's house.
'That Ogre frightens everyone in the village,'
says Daniel to his cat. 'I don't like him.'
'Look!' says Daniel's cat. 'There's Princess
Caroline in her coach. You like her!'

Princess Caroline smiles at Daniel.
'Yes, I do,' says Daniel. 'She's very
beautiful. How can I meet her?'
'I've got an idea,' says his cat.

'I can go to the King's palace with some presents from you,' says Daniel's cat.
'But I'm a poor man,' says Daniel. 'I can't buy presents for the King.'

'No,' says his cat. 'But we can catch some fish for the King.'

Daniel and his cat go to the river and catch four big fish. 'Now give me a pair of boots and a hat with a feather,' says Daniel's cat.

'You look very handsome with your new boots and hat,' says Daniel.
'Good! Now I'm ready to meet the King!' says the cat.

'What can I call you when I meet the King?' says the cat. 'I can't call you Daniel… can I call you Lord Carabas?' 'Yes,' says Daniel. 'That's an excellent name. And I can call you Puss in Boots!'

Puss in Boots puts the fish in his bag and goes to the King's palace.

'Good morning, your Majesty,' he says. 'I've got four big fish in my bag. A present from Lord Carabas.'

'What beautiful big fish! Thank you very much!' says the King. 'Lord Carabas is very kind. When can I meet him?'

'Soon,' says Puss in Boots. 'Very soon.'

The next day Puss in Boots sees the King's coach near the river.

'Quickly, Daniel, jump into the river!' he says.

'I can't jump into the river,' says Daniel. 'I can't swim!'

'Look! The King's coming in his coach,' says Puss in Boots. 'He can help you.'

'Help! Please help!' says Puss in Boots. 'Lord Carabas is in the river and he can't swim!'

'Stop the coach!' says the King.

'You're cold and wet,' says the King. 'Please come to the palace with me. I can give you some dry clothes. Then I can take you home in my coach.'

'Thank you, your Majesty. You're very kind!' says Daniel.

'That's an excellent idea,' says Puss in Boots. 'Lord Carabas's castle is over there. I can go to the castle and make tea for everyone!'

Puss in Boots goes to the ugly Ogre's castle.

He knocks on the door.

'Who's knocking on my door?' says the Ogre. 'Go away!'

'Please open the door,' says Puss in Boots. 'Everyone in the village says that you have magic powers. I'm a magic cat and I want to meet you.'

The Ogre wants to meet the magic cat. He opens the door.

'Please come in,' he says.

'Everyone in the village says you can change into an animal,' says Puss in Boots. 'Can you change into a big animal? A big lion?'
'OF COURSE I CAN!' says the Ogre. 'I can change into a lion and eat you!

The Ogre frightens Puss in Boots.

'No, no! Please don't eat me!' says Puss in Boots.

'I'm a magic cat and I can eat you!'

'You can't eat me!' says the Ogre. 'Small cats can't eat big Ogres!'

'No, of course small cats can't eat big Ogres,' says Puss in Boots.

'Your magic powers are excellent! You can change into a big lion but... can you change into a small mouse?'

'OF COURSE I CAN!' says the Ogre.

'Excellent!' says Puss in Boots. 'Small cats can't eat big Ogres but... they can eat small mice!'

Puss in Boots looks out of the window.
The King, the Queen, Princess Caroline and Daniel are coming into the castle.
'You've got a very beautiful castle,' says the King.
'Thank you,' says Daniel.
'And you've got a very beautiful daughter.'

They have tea.

Princess Caroline smiles at Daniel.

Daniel is very happy.

'Your Majesty,' he says to the King. 'I want to marry Princess Caroline.'

'And I want to marry Lord Carabas,' says Princess Caroline.

Yes or no?

1 Read the sentences and look at the pictures. Write 'yes' or 'no'.

Example: Puss in Boots catches five fish.   .No.

1 Puss in Boots calls Daniel 'Lord Daniel'.   ......
2 Princess Caroline smiles at Daniel's cat.   ......
3 Daniel can't swim.   ......
4 The King takes Daniel to his palace.   ......
5 Puss in Boots goes to the Ogre's castle.   ......
6 The Ogre is beautiful.   ......
7 The Ogre changes into a lion.   ......
8 Small cats can't eat small mice.   ......

'C' words

2 Circle the right words in these sentences.

Example:
Puss in Boots and Daniel (catch)/come four fish.

1 The Ogre lives in a beautiful castle/coach.
2 'I've got an idea,' says Daniel's cat/coach.
3 'Stop the cat/coach!' says the King.
4 'You're clothes/cold and wet,' says the King.
'Please catch/come to the palace with me. I
can give you some dry change/clothes'.

**Now unscramble the words in the wheel.
All the words begin with 'c' and they are all
in the sentences above.**

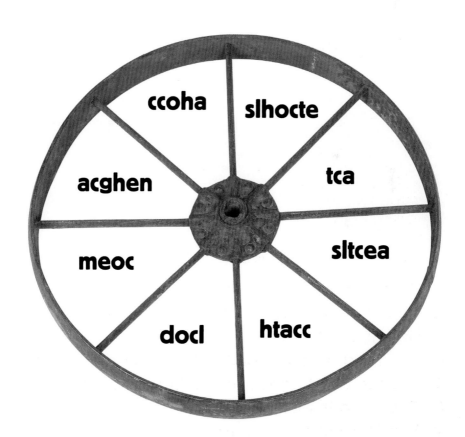

ccoha   slhocte

acghen   tca

meoc   sltcea

docl   htacc

Join

3 Join the pictures to the right words.

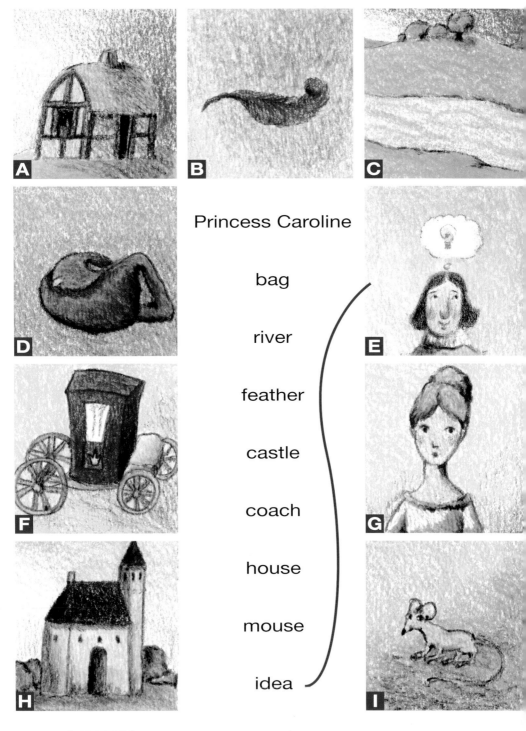

Princess Caroline

bag

river

feather

castle

coach

house

mouse

idea

Write the correct words in the sentences.

Example: Puss in Boots has got an ...idea............ .

1 The Ogre lives in a ....
2 Daniel lives in a small ....
3 Puss in Boots has got a .... in his hat.
4 Puss in Boots puts the fish in his ....
5 Daniel jumps into the ....
6 The King's coming in his ....
7 The Ogre changes into a lion and a ....
8 Daniel wants to marry ....

Whose are these?

**4 Join the person to the correct picture.
Then complete the sentences.**

Daniel's

The King's

Puss in Boots's

Princess Caroline's

The Ogre's

Example: .The Ogre's..... castle.
1 .... bag.
2 .... palace.
3 .... coach.
4 .... cat.

Find the words in the balls

5 Join a blue ball and a yellow ball to make a
word.

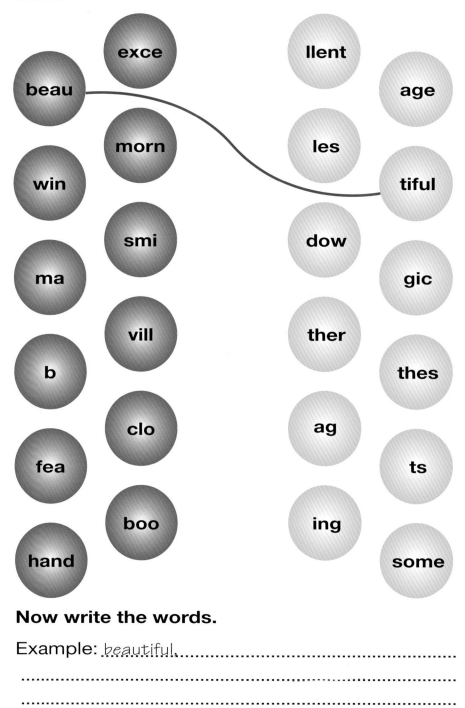

Now write the words.

Example: beautiful...

....

....

Cut-out Puss in Boots

6 Use the lines on page 28 to cut out the pieces.
Put the clothes on
Puss in Boots.

Picture Dictionary

King :

Queen :

Princess :

Ogre :

man :

animals :

cat :

fish :

lion :

mouse :

mice :

palace :

castle :

house :

door :

window :

coach :

river :

village :

bag :

boots :

clothes :

feather :

hat :

presents :

bad :

beautiful :

dry :　wet :

handsome :

ugly :

big :　small :

cold :

happy :

catch a fish :

change into :

30

Key

Activity 1: 1 no; **2** no; **3** yes; **4** yes; **5** yes; **6** no; **7** yes; **8** no.

Activity 2: 1 castle; **2** cat; **3** coach; **4** cold; come; clothes.

'C' words: catch, come, cold, castle, cat, clothes, change, coach.

Activity 3: 1 castle (H); **2** house (A); **3** feather (B); **4** bag (D); **5** river (C); **6** coach (F); **7** mouse (I); **8** Princess Caroline (G).

Activity 4: 1 Puss in Boots's bag. (D) **2** The King's palace. (A) **3** Princess Caroline's coach. (C) **4** Daniel's cat (E)

Activity 5: excellent, handsome, morning, smiles, village, window, clothes, magic, feather, boots, bag.

swim :

stop :

smile :

open :

meet :

marry :

: knock

jump :

help :

have tea :

go :

give :

frighten :

eat :

Editor: Robert Hill

Design and art direction: Nadia Maestri

Computer graphics: Simona Corniola

© 2008   Black Cat Publishing,
         an imprint of Cideb Editrice, Genoa, Canterbury

First edition: March 2008

We would be happy to receive your comments and suggestions,
and give you any other information concerning our material.
editorial@blackcat-cideb.com
www.blackcat-cideb.com / www.cideb.it

CISQ CISQ CERT
TEXTBOOKS AND
TEACHING MATERIALS
The quality of the publisher's
design, production and sales processes has
been certified to the standard of
UNI EN ISO 9001

ISBN 978-88-530-0693-6

Printed in Italy by Litoprint, Genoa